PRANKS GAGS and JOKES

PRANKS GAGS AND JOKES

By AnnMarie MacKinnon

Illustrated by Michael Kline

First published in 2010
by SpiceBox™
3918 Kitchener Street
Burnaby, BC Canada
V5C 3M2
www.spicebox.ca

ISBN 10: 1-926567-15-3
ISBN13: 978-1-926567-15-0

CEO and Publisher: Ben Lotfi
Editor: AnnMarie MacKinnon
Creative Director: Garett Chan
Art Director: Christine Covert
Designer: Leslie Irvine
Production: James Badger
Sourcing: Janny Lam

Original illustrations
Michael Kline (dogfoose.com)

Printed in China

TABLE OF CONTENTS

Introduction

Who doesn't love to be the person waiting around the corner for a helpless victim to fall prey to your trap? Everyone loves a bit of mischief and there are as many ways to play a prank as there are people to play them on. You'll find tonnes of sure-fire ways to get people laughing, whether you catch them with one of the gags or tickle their funny bone with some of the jokes.

April Fool's Day will never be the same!

What is a Practical Joke?

A practical joke is a situation that's set up by the prankster to make the victim of the joke (called a "mark") look silly or feel embarrassed. The "practical" part comes from having some sort of action or practice involved, rather than just telling or writing a joke. Practical jokes can be simple, like putting a Whoopee cushion on the mark's chair, or can be very elaborate, involving hidden cameras to catch the action. Whatever kind of practical joke you opt for, make sure it's safe.

RememBer:

There can be consequences to pulling pranks—you might just start a prank war! If you pull a gag on someone else, make sure you're ready for the revenge prank.

When to Play a Practical Joke

April Fool's Day is the obvious choice for pulling one over on your friends, and Hallowe'en is a close second. But is there really a bad day for a joke? A good laugh is almost always welcome. A good-natured prank can brighten a friend's mood if they're grumpy and can do wonders for your popularity at school.

When **Not** to Play a Practical Joke

Unless you're hoping to make enemies, don't play any practical jokes when your mark has a big day coming up. You don't want to see the wrath that can ensue when your mom comes out of the shower on the day of her big presentation at work when you've doctored the soap with food coloring!

Make sure your pranks are safe and won't cause harm. Jokes that leave permanent damage like ruining someone's clothes or personal belongings just aren't funny. If you set up a gag that makes a mess, make sure you stick around to help clean it up. It's only fair, and it gives you a reputation as a good prankster, instead of just a brat.

Keep your practical jokes playful and friendly. Practical jokes are supposed to be fun—for everyone. The goal of being a prankster is to get everyone into the spirit of things, not to make people feel hurt or humiliated. Keep them laughing (and guessing)!

Setting the Scene

With all good practical jokes comes a little preparation. After all, everything has to be in place so that you can really enjoy the look on your mark's face when he finally clues in to what's going on. Here are some of the tricks of the trade when it comes to setting up your prank.

Choose Your Mark Wisely

A gag is always funniest when played on someone who can laugh at herself and appreciates a well-told joke. Chances are if she's played a practical joke herself, she'll make an excellent mark. People who are really shy or embarrass easily just won't enjoy being the centre of attention. Make them your accomplice instead!

Acting and Delivery

The element of surprise is crucial to a successful joke, so act like nothing's going on. Just be yourself and try not to burst out laughing before the punch line.

Timing is Everything

The key to being a successful jokester is knowing when to deliver the punch line. Give your audience the chance to react to the joke before saying anything or moving on to the next joke. Take the time to enjoy the mark's reaction. You'll have plenty of time to giggle at it later.

Hiding

You're going to want front row seats to watch your mark's reaction to your practical joke, so unless you're able to keep a straight face really well, you'll need a hiding spot. Choose wisely. Set yourself up in a spot where you can clearly see the action, but won't be seen by your mark and give anything away.

Using Co-Conspirators

This can be a great way to pull off a more complicated prank, or to just let a few more people in on the joke. When choosing a co-conspirator, make sure that he can keep a straight face and not give the joke away too soon. For certain practical jokes, it's better if the co-conspirator is someone the mark doesn't know, making the scenario all the more unexpected and effective.

Where Does April Fool's Day Come from?

There are a few theories as to how April Fool's Day first started, but most of them have to do with changing over from the Julian calendar (named after Julius Caesar) to the Gregorian calendar (the same calendar we use today) in the Middle Ages. According to the Julian calendar, New Year's Day was on April 1st. When the calendar changed, New Year's Day was changed to January 1st, but some people still used the April 1st date. These people were called "April fools".

In France, April Fool's Day is called "Poisson d'Avril" and schoolchildren secretly tape paper fish to their friend's backs. When the victim of the joke discovers they've been walking around with a fish on his or her back, the other kids yell "Poisson d'Avril!" or "April fish".

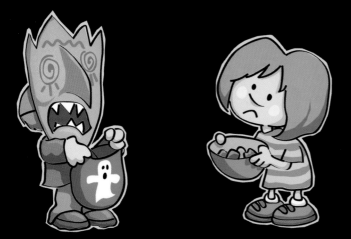

Why Do We Say "trick or treat" on Hallowe'en?

Though trick-or-treating as we know it is a relatively new phenomenon, its history is thought to date back over 2000 years. The ancient Celts (as well as other cultures such as the Chinese and Egyptians) believed that spirits required food and drink just like the living. On October 31st, the end of summer, the souls of the dead traveled to visit the living. Food and drink was left out for the spirits to consume on their journey. It was believed that people who did not make an offering left themselves open to mischief (or tricks) from the spirits.

The Practical Jokes

The Arm in the GarBage

What You'll Need
An old shirt
A work glove
(or some other kind of glove)
Newspaper for stuffing
A sewing needle and thread
or fabric glue

Take an old shirt and cut one of the sleeves off at the shoulder. Tuck the cuff end of the sleeve inside the opening of the glove and sew or glue it in place. Stuff the glove and the sleeve with balled up newspaper. Try to make it look like as life-like as possible by making sure there are no big bumps. You can also pose the hands by curling the fingers a little. Once you've finished stuffing, sew up the other end to avoid losing your stuffing.

Next time the trash is at the curb for pick up, place the arm so it's hanging outside of the trash can with the lid resting on top of it and watch for the double takes and raised eyebrows!

Some other great things to do with the arm are to "slam" it in a car door, so that it hangs outside the car. You can also place it in the fridge for a great surprise for anyone going to fetch that late night snack. The arm works like a charm wherever it is least expected!

When you're cutting the sleeve off the shirt, make sure it's an old one no one needs anymore!

Gift With Strings Attached

No one can resist a beautifully decorated gift. And you won't be able to resist laughing at this gag! It works great on neighbors or on your family.

What You'll Need

A box
Some gift wrap and ribbon
A length of clear nylon fishing line
An accomplice

Wrap up a box so that it looks like a beautiful present. Tie the length of fishing line to the ribbon at the back of the box. Have your accomplice place it outside of a neighbor's door, knock or ring the doorbell, then run away. When your neighbor opens the door, they'll be thrilled to find a gift just for them. When they reach down, all smiles, to pick it up, pull the string, tugging the gift just out of their reach. Watch their surprised expression and giggle.

JOKES

Q: What's the best way to catch a monkey?
A: Climb a tree and act like **a banana.**

Q: What do you call James Bond in the bath?
A: Bubble 07!

Q: What has wheels **and a trunk** but no engine?
A: An elephant on rollerskates.

Q: Where do snowmen keep their money?
A: In snowbanks.

Superglued Coins

This one is a beauty—some people will spend ages trying to save a quarter!

What You'll Need
A few coins
Some superglue
A good hiding spot

The set-up for this prank is simple. Find a place with lots of people walking by, like near a school or library. Place a little dab of superglue on a coin and stick it to the ground. Find a hiding spot and watch people try to pick up the coin in vain. This is extra fun if you take pictures!

Remember: Superglue is very, very sticky. Even on skin! We recommend that you get the help of an adult with a good sense of humor to help you safely handle the glue so the joke's not on you.

The Empty Box

This joke depends entirely on your acting skills. Practice in front of a mirror a few times before you try it out for real.

What You'll Need

An empty box or container you can't see through

Come into a room carrying your box or container as if it's very heavy. Set it down on a table, making sure it appears that the container has weight in it. A moment later, ask someone to pass it to you. Thinking that it is heavy, they'll pick it up with more force than is necessary, and the box will shoot up!

Balloon closet

This is a great prank to do on
someone's birthday
but it can work any time.

What You'll Need

Balloons
Lots of air
Some time to place the balloons
while no one's looking

Blow up lots and lots of balloons. This
could take a while so give yourself
lots of time, or enlist the help of an
accomplice. Find a cupboard or closet
to fill, then wait to see the reaction
when the balloons spill out when the
door is opened. Another great place to
do this is behind the shower curtain,
so that when someone tries to get in,
they're "showered" with balloons.

Use garbage bags to help you put the balloons in place instead of trying to put them in the closet one at a time. Just fill up the garbage bags with your inflated balloons. Put them in the closet, with the opening of the bag facing the back of the closet. Close the door, leaving only enough room for you to stick your arm in and grab the end of the bag. When you pull the bag out, the balloons will stay inside—just shut the door quickly!

The Green Cow

This will surprise anyone trying to have their cereal in the morning!

What You'll Need

A few drops of green food coloring

If your milk comes in a cardboard carton, place a few drops of the food coloring, and give the carton a gentle shake to mix it in. Wait for someone to get the milk out of the fridge for their cereal and watch their face!

JOKES

Q: What does a tree do when he is ready to go home?
A: He leaves.

Q: Why did the burglar take a bath?
A: He wanted to make a clean getaway.

Q: What's smarter than a talking horse?
A: A spelling bee.

Q: What is a bee's favorite classical music composer?
A: Bee-thoven!

Q: What did the skeletons say before dinner?
A: Bone appetit!

21

Infinite Thread

This one gets looks of confusion, then the laugh.

What You'll Need
A spool of thread

Put a spool of thread in your pocket (preferably the same color as your clothing) and let the end of the thread hang out. Show the end of the thread to a friend and tell them you've been pulling at the thread all day, but can't seem to get rid of it. Ask them if they'll help. They'll find they can pull and pull all day, but all they get is a handful of thread.

The OlD SWitCheroo

This is an oldie, but a goodie. It's so much fun to watch people searching for their belongings!

What You'll Need

A little time to move things around

This one works best when your mark is going to be out of the house for a while. Just go into a room they don't use frequently and move things around. For example, switch their dresser drawers so that the socks that were in the top drawer are switched with the t-shirts from the bottom drawer. Or, in the kitchen, you can move around the pots and pans from their usual spots. Try the joke in different rooms each time.

TaPe It UP

Observe as your mark struggles to get dressed.

What You'll Need
Double-sided tape

When your mark isn't looking, tape up the cuffs of shirtsleeves and pant legs on the inside. Fold the clothes neatly so that no one will suspect what's happening. When they try to get dressed, your mark will have more trouble than usual putting on clothes.

unDerwear caper

Laundry day has never been so fun.

What You'll Need

Lots of safety pins

Sneak into your brother's room and go directly to his underwear drawer. Pin all the pairs of underwear together, so that when he pulls a pair out, they all come out in a long chain. After pinning them together, be sure to fold them so they look like they haven't been tampered with.

JOKES

Q: When do kangaroos **celebrate** their birthdays?
A: During leap year!

Q: What do you call a pig that does karate?
A: Pork Chop!

Q: What do you call **a cat** with eight legs.
A: An octopuss!

Q: Why did the painting **go to jail?**
A: Because it was framed.

Q: Why did the cat sit on the computer?
A: To keep an eye on the mouse.

Unrippable Toilet Paper

Another great bathroom caper, this one will have your mark stranded until he or she figures out how to get some of the paper off the roll.

What You'll Need

A roll of toilet paper
Some cellophane tape

Unroll some of the toilet paper and tape it on the under side so the tape won't be visible. Roll the toilet paper back up. The next person who tries to use it will find they'll need a little extra force in order to tear the toilet roll.

The Very Mysterious Cake

Sneaking a slice of this cake might be a little more complicated...

What You'll Need

An empty cereal box
Icing

Frost the cereal box with icing. You could even write a message in a different color icing to make it look more authentic. Let your marks know there's cake up for grabs and watch them try to slice it.

The Strange Bowl of Cereal

This peculiar breakfast works really well on the extra sleepy member of your family who is not a morning person.

What You'll Need

A bowl of water

The night before your prank, fill a bowl about half full of water and freeze it solid. In the morning, pour a thin layer of cereal and milk on top and laugh while your mark tries to dig into a healthy, nutritious breakfast of ice.

This Soap is Broken

Rub the soap as long as you want!
There won't be any bubbles.

What You'll Need

A new bar of soap
A bottle of clear nail polish

Paint the entire surface of a bar of soap with clear nail polish, and let it dry. Place the soap out for use and wait for someone to try to use it. They'll wet the soap and try to lather it up, but it just won't work!

You might want to have an adult help you with this one—it can be messy!

JOKES

Q:Why was six afraid of seven?

A:Because seven eight nine!

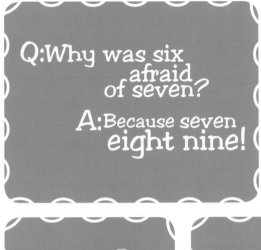

Q: What is the most slippery country in the world?

A: Greece.

Q: Why did the bacon laugh?
A: Because the egg cracked a yolk.

Q: Why did the otter **cross** the road?

A: To get to the otter side.

Q: Why was the broom late?
A: It over-swept.

31

Sleeping Beauty

Your mark should be a sound sleeper to make this one work.

What You'll Need

Whipped cream
A feather

Wait until your mark is sound asleep (preferably snoring) and has one hand exposed. As they slumber, fill their hand with the whipped cream. Next, take the feather and tickle their nose gently. Your mark will think a fly is tickling them and will try to swat it away—with the hand filled with whipped cream!

The salt Switcheroo

This is a classic prank that works every time!

What you'll need
Salt and Sugar

This is a really simple prank to pull off. Just switch the salt with the sugar and watch the reaction when Mom or Dad puts salt in their coffee or sugar on their dinner.

Don't even think of doing this in large scale, like switching the ingredients when someone is baking a cake. That is a recipe for disaster!

Plastic Wrap Shenanigan

This is a quick way to get some very confused looks in the kitchen or at the dinner table.

What You'll Need

Plastic wrap
Salt and paper shakers

Take the lid off the salt and pepper shakers. Cover each opening with a small piece of plastic wrap, taking care that no wrap shows when you replace the covers. At dinner, you'll see someone shake those salt and pepper shakers.

A variation on this classic is to put a small indent in the plastic wrap and pour some salt or pepper on top before replacing the lid. Imagine your mark's surprise when a healthy dose of pepper comes out of the salt shaker.

The Toilet Paper Trick

This surprise will definitely take place when your mark is least expecting it.

What You'll Need

Toilet paper
A marker

Unroll part of the toilet paper and write messages on a few of the sheets. Roll up the toilet tissue and wait. Write your own message or try "Help, I'm trapped in a toilet paper factory!"

JOKES

Q: What happened to the leopard who took **four** baths every day?
A: Within a week **he was spotless.**

Q: What medicine would you give **an ill ant?**

A: Antibiotics!

Q: What do you call an elephant that flies?
A: A jumbo jet.

Q: If an athlete gets athlete's foot, what does an astronaut get?
A: Missile toe.

Q: If you have 9 oranges in one hand, and 10 lemons in the other hand, what do you have?
A: Really big hands!

cereal Box Switch

See how long it takes for anyone to notice they're not eating the cereal they thought they were.

What You'll Need

Several boxes of different kinds of cereal

Switch the inside liner bags of cereal so that each cereal is in the wrong box. Sleepyheads might take a while to realize they're having bran flakes instead of corn flakes.

Ready for the Test

Watching the panic in your friend's eyes is priceless.

What You'll Need

An accomplice

Walk into the classroom and ask your friend if he's ready for the big quiz today. If your friend is suspicious, ask your accomplice to confirm your story as back up. Let the cramming begin!

The Force Field

This prank is pure gold, especially if you catch someone who's in a rush to go somewhere.

What You'll Need

A roll of plastic wrap or clear cellophane tape

Completely cover a doorway with plastic wrap or tape. Take care that the plastic doesn't overlap, making it more visible. Also make sure you do this on a door that opens inward.

You can also do this prank by only placing tape or plastic wrap near the bottom of the door to make your mark trip. Just make sure there are no dangerous obstacles around!

JOKES

Q: What dog loves to take bubble baths?
A: A shampoodle.

Q: What did one eye say to the other?
A: Between you and me, something smells.

Q: What is the difference between a flea and a wolf?
A: One prowls on the hairy and the other howls on the prairie!

Q: Did you hear about the man who got his left side cut off?
A: He's all right now.

Q: Why are elephants wrinkled?
A: Have you ever tried to iron one?

40

The Incredible Shrinking Shoes

This prank always gets looks of confusion from people who think either their feet grew or their shoes have shrunk.

What You'll Need

Stuffing such as cotton balls or newspaper

When no one is around, stuff the toes of people's shoes with paper or cotton and wait for them to try to put them on. It will be hard not to start laughing as you see your victim struggle to put on the shoes that just yesterday fit perfectly.

A Refreshing Drink

This is a really simple prank that works immediately.

What You'll Need

Vinegar

When your mark leaves her refreshing glass of water unattended, drop in some vinegar and wait. It's so sour, that your mark's face will pucker up as soon as she tastes the "new flavor" you've added to her drink.

Don't Cry Over Spilled Milk

This prank takes a little bit of preparation but is totally worth it.

What You'll Need

Waxed paper

A drinking glass

Paint (that same color as your favorite drink)

Put some paint the same color as your favorite drink (brown for chocolate milk, orange for orange juice, for example) into your drinking glass. Gently tip the glass on its side to allow some of the paint to run out onto the waxed paper. Let this dry so that you can pick the glass up and peel the paint off the waxed paper while keeping it attached to the glass.

Next time you're having a drink, quickly switch the glasses when no one is looking and watch someone try to clean up your "spill".

43

Broomstick Trick

This one will leave your mark scratching his head for a while trying to figure out how to get out of it.

What You'll Need

A glass of water
A broomstick

Stand on a chair and hold a full glass of water against the ceiling. Ask your mark to help you with a science experiment (if they ask what it's about, say "physics"). Tell them to hold the glass of water against the ceiling with the broomstick. Walk away, leaving them wondering how to get the glass down without it spilling everywhere.

JOKES

Q: What game do elephants play with ants?
A: Squash!

Q: What did one tomato say to the other?
A: You go on ahead and I'll ketchup!

Q: What do you call a bee that is always complaining? A: A grumble bee!

Q: What goes ha ha ha plop?
A: Someone laughing their head off!

Q: Why did the banana go to the doctor?
A: He wasn't peeling well!

Bedroom Tug of War

Ah, sibling rivalry. Where would the prankster be without it?

What You'll Need

piece of string or rope long enough
to reach between two doors with a

Choose two doors that are close together, or across the hall from one another. Make sure there are people inside each room. Take the rope and tie an end to each doorknob tightly, leaving a little bit of slack in the middle. When the doors are secured, knock on both and watch the tug of

Rrrrriip!

A Rip Roaring Good Time

Embarrassment ensues when this prank is pulled on an unsuspecting mark.

What You'll Need

An easy-to-tear piece of fabric and some money

Place some money on the floor in an obvious location. Find a nearby hiding spot and wait. Your mark will walk by and spot the money. When they bend over to pick it up, tear the fabric loudly from your hiding spot. Your victim will panic and check their rear when they think they've torn their pants by bending over.

"Rain" Storm

Choose a rainy day for this one!

What You'll Need

An umbrella
Lots of glitter or confetti

When the umbrella is resting with the handle
pointing up, fill the umbrella with glitter or confetti.
When your mark goes out and opens the umbrella,
the confetti will create a shower of its own.

JOKES

Q: How do you make **a milk shake?**
A: Give it a good scare.

Q: **What do you get if you cross a duck with a firework?**
A: **A fire-quacker.**

Q: Why did the turkey cross the road?
A: It was the chicken's **day off.**

Q: **What do you get when you cross an elephant with a fish?**
A: **Swimming trunks.**

Q: What did the hat say to the scarf?
A: You hang around while I go on ahead!

49

uck on you

...n wreak all sorts of havoc with
...ssages you decide to print on
these stickers.

What You'll Need
Blank computer labels

...ither on your computer or

labels. You can go with the tr...
'kick me' or 'teacher's pet' st...
something a little more origin...
choice is up to you. When you...
suspects nothing, give them a...
or pat on the back, sticking th...

A Nutty Message

What You'll Need
Some walnuts
Small slips of paper with messages
on them
Superglue

Crack open the nuts into two halves along the seam, taking care not to shatter the shells. Remove the nut from the inside and replace it with a note, a fortune, a gummy worm, fake bug, or some other strange object. Glue the two shell halves back together, then leave for your mark to find. They'll get a surprise when they try to have a snack.

Have an adult help you with cracking the nuts and using superglue to put them back together.

JOKES

Q: **What birds steal the soap from your bath?**
A: **Robber ducks.**

Q: Why do golfers always carry an extra **pair of socks?** A: In case they get a hole in one!

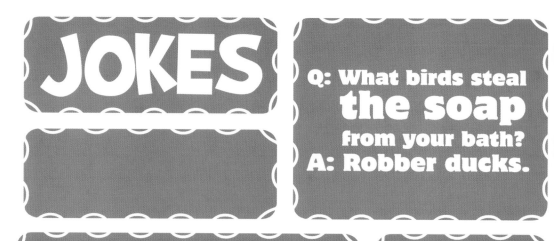

Q: Why did the nurse **tip-toe past** the medicine cabinet? A: Because she didn't want to wake the **sleeping pills.**

Q: Where do ghosts go to become pilots? A: Fright-school.

Q: What are prehistoric monsters called when they sleep? A: Dino-snores!

Towel Trickery

A relaxing day at the beach turns tricky...

What You'll Need

Your hands
A little time

There's nothing more relaxing than drying off on your towel at the beach on a sunny day. When your beach companion steps away for a minute, dig a hole in the sand underneath where their towel was laying, then replace the towel before they get back. When your mark goes to lie back down to work on their tan, they'll sink a little deeper than they expected.

The Short Sheet

This prank is a timeless classic...

What You'll Need

Time to mess with someone's bed undetected

While your hapless mark is away, sneak into his room and make his bed for him. He won't be very happy about the favor when he tries to crawl into bed. Leave the fitted sheet (the one the fits snugly around the mattress) where it is and take the top flat sheet and spread it out over the bed. At the head of the bed, tuck the fitted sheet under the mattress neatly. Pull the bottom end of the sheet up to where the top would normally be, then place the blankets on top. Fold down the end of the sheet for an extra tidy "freshly made" look.

The End